Wild Spirit of the Living God

Russ Parker

Wild Spirit of the Living God

Prayer poems for the journey

Rev. Dr Russ Parker

eagle

Eagle Publishing, Bath

This edition, © 2007 Eagle Publishing Ltd, 3-4 The Drove, West Wilts Trading Estate, Westbury, Wiltshire, BA13 4JE.

British Library Cataloguing in Publication Data. A catalogue record for this book is available from the British Library.

Typeset by Eagle Publishing Ltd
Printed by CPD
ISBN No: 978 0 86347 633 4

Dedication

I dedicate this anthology to my wife Roz who was the very first person I had the courage to read my poems to. She has always believed in me even when I was in no position to do so myself.

Contents

Foreword

We are not as imaginative in prayer as we could be. It often seems, both in my own prayer life, and in the extempore communal prayers of the church, that inspiration gives way to a jumble of rambling phrases. Yet the Scripture writers, from Moses to the Psalmist, the Apostle Paul or the much-loved John, all conversed with the Almighty in some of the most beautiful words and memorable ways available to them. Their prayer poems have stayed with us, fed and sustained us for generations.

So thank heavens for Russ Parker, a contemporary voice in the great biblical and spiritual tradition of prayer poets. Russ is a man for whom prayer matters so much that it must be the very best he has to offer, and that is his poetry, for poetry is the vehicle that best lends itself to expressing the deepest heart cry, the greatest longings, the unfathomable mystery and sudden, overwhelming sense of wonder, grace and glory that fill the human spirit. These poems are fresh and vivid, immediate and alluring. But be warned, they're not just an easy read. Russ takes us into the secret place of his own journey with God, and it often feels, as we read them, as if we're treading on holy ground. We plummet the depths and hit the heights of human experience, and the road from one to the other can be uncomfortable, as the superficial niceness attached to much of the communication that passes for prayer is stripped away and replaced with raw and real emotion.

No one is perhaps better equipped to write in this way than Russ. Both personal experience, and his many years as the Director of the Acorn Christian Healing Foundation, have given him a profound insight into the self-doubt and bewilderment that afflicts the human spirit. After all, he's a Scouse by background, a child of those swinging sixties in a Merseyside that produced a wealth of talented songwriters, dramatists and poets, including Willy Russell and the Beatles. He too has always been a free spirit, unfettered by convention, dissatisfied with the status quo, saddened when human beings are prevented from reaching their God-given potential, all underpinned with a gentle, self-deprecating, sense of humour. It was in Liverpool he learnt that the dogmas that divide Christians are artificial, that there are lessons to learn from both fiery Protestantism and quiet Catholicism, and that the best in both traditions can be invigorating and enriching.

Russ went on to work in a variety of very ordinary jobs, made extraordinary by his encounters with people whose lives he touched in his own inimitable way. When his ministry became official, he never allowed his professionalism or academic prowess to curb his inner freedom or clip the wings of his imagination. He's never less than ruthlessly honest about his own difficult journey through pain to new joy. Meeting Russ is always a revelation. He never does or says what anyone expects. And he remains one of the best story-tellers I have ever met.

These are the influences that have prepared and polished the gems in this treasure chest. Here are the years of seeking, listening, questioning, doubting, hurting, learning, loving and wondering, of personal soul-searching, and of empathy with the hundreds who have sought his ministry either at Whitehill Chase, Acorn's HQ in Hampshire or on his many travels. Here is comfort in pain, encouragement in indecision, support in bewilderment, reassurance in doubt, challenge in self-pity, and a glimpse of the everlasting joy and peace that is there for all the battle-weary pilgrims.

Russ stretches our praying beyond where it normally stops. But would the wild, untamed, all-knowing Holy Spirit of God expect anything less than ruthless honesty? He once wrote one of his own inimitable dedications in a book to us, "He is wild, but he won't hurt you." I've never forgotten that phrase. It captures the essence of the Aslan-like God Russ knows, loves and trusts, who takes us by the hand and gently leads us upwards and onwards to some of the scarier, but wonderful places we have never visited before.

There is an almost Celtic flow and rhythm to the prayer poems that make them memorable, so that the more they are read, the more treasure they yield. Whether they are used publicly or privately, and I will use them for both, they will feed and strengthen us, and make us rethink and revise our own prayer journey. It takes the creativity of the poet to release our own imagination in prayer. That is Russ' gift to us, for once it happens, we will never be satisfied with anything less.

Michele Guinness

The Wild Spirit

Wild Spirit, Wild Wind.

Lord God of the wild wind of heaven,
Send us your warm wind,
Your fresh wind,
Your mighty wind;
It's what we want for Jesus' sake.

Amen

Restoration

Wild Spirit of the living God
be the calm in my storm,
the light in my dark;
the One who believes in me
even when I don't.

Wild Spirit of the raised up Son,
be the healer of my hurt,
the holder of my hand;
the One who seeks better things for me
even when I can't.

Light the lion's flame of passion in me,
give me the giving heart
of heaven's holy warrior
so that I learn to bc still
    to be stopped,
    to recover,
    to be released,
    to be renewed
through Jesus Christ,
the bloodied but victorious lamb.

    Amen

Servant Heart

Wild Spirit of the living God,
breathe the breath of heaven's lion
into this timid soul of mine.
Shape me by the touch of the crucified lamb,
so that I carry the cross
with the dignity of a crown.
Wrap my fears in the faith you have in me,
and help me to lean into your blowing winds,
stand in the gaps of your calling,
fall under the weight of grace,
speak to mountains in your name,
go quietly to the secret place of prayer
give away my gifts that others may grow
and in steps hardly noticed,
be changed forever into your likeness
through Jesus Christ my Lord.
Amen

Dreamer's Prayer

Wild Spirit of the living God,
Make a dreamer out of me.
Step into my sleep
And call me to new adventures
On the tides of your turning grace.
Let my night times
Be changed and charged
With the dawning day of new insights.
Let my resting in the dark
Leading to dancing in the blazing morning
Of new revelations of the depths
And layers of your care
For the whole of me,
Sleeping and awake.
Let the ending of the day
Lead to glimpses
Of one like the son of man
Whose face is like the shining sun
In all its brilliance.
Amen.

The Path I Tread

Wild Spirit of the living God,
bless to me the path I tread,
when I should stop
and where I should go;
let your welcome presence
help me to know
the time to be silent,
the time to scream.
Let there be places
where I can doubt and dream.
Let these be moments
when I am shaped
as a true child
of the scarred and wounded king.

Amen

The Rhythm of Renewal

O Holy Spirit of the living God,
In my life
Be wild and free;
Uphold me and upset me,
Strengthen me and weaken me,
Stop me and stir me,
Waken me and rest me,
Teach me and test me,
Make me more like Christ,
Make me fully human,
Whether it be the cross or the crown
May your mercy and your might
Flood me and fill me
So that I long for God all the more.

Amen

Vision Prayer

Wild Spirit of the living God
fall afresh on me.
Give me the eye of the eagle
so that I can see what is far off
and pray,
"thy kingdom come nearer,
thy kingdom come more powerfully,
thy kingdom come on earth as it is in heaven,
thy kingdom come now."

Amen

Growing Up, Going On

Wild Spirit of the living God,
Teach me to go through life
The right way around,
To be so secure
In whom I am rather
Than in what I do.
Give me moments of
Cradling quiet
So that I can be restored.
Let me hear your lion's roar
And fill my heart with exaltation.
Be the still small voice for me
So that I come out of shadow
Into your sunshine.
Heal the hurting child in me
So that I can go on growing up
And live in the power of your
Kingdom presence.
Amen

I Want to See You

Wild Spirit of my nights and days,
wake me up with your word of life
so that I might see you,
so that I might serve you.

Jesus Christ, bright and morning star
shine on the highways of my heart
so that I might see you
so that I might serve you.

Great God of waiting and wonders
weave your threads of healing in me
so that I might see you,
so that I might serve you,
so that I might celebrate you,
my Lord and my God.
Amen

Being There

Wild Spirit of the living God,
Make me cool waters
In someone else's parched land;
A sheltered place for the fallen
A haven for the wounded;
A safe place for the frightened
A highway for the wanderer;
A still place for the fugitive
A home for the weary;
A strong place for the feeble
And a hill for thc oncs
who want to see further.
Wild Spirit of the living God,
Give me a listening heart
instead of an informed mind
So that I meet someone else's need
Rather than my own,
Through Jesus Christ my Lord,
Amen

Grab me God

Wild Spirit of the living, breathing God
Come and get me,
Come and grab me,
Come and get a hold of me.
I don't want to manage without you anymore.

Wild Spirit of the living, breathing God
Do your deep work,
Do your best work
Do what's in your heart to do,
I don't want the thin, unchallenged life anymore.

Wild Spirit of the living, breathing God
Don't go,
Don't leave,
Don't be the unseen observer, silent listener.
I don't want to be safe but sorry anymore.

Wild Spirit of the living, breathing God
Send your Spirit,
Send him more powerfully,
Send him now.
I don't want to be anywhere else anymore.

Healings on the Journey

I Turn Home

Leader When I am lost and need to find my way…
All I turn home.

Leader When I am hurt and want to find healing…
All I turn home.

Leader When I am at the cross-roads and don't know which way to turn..
All I turn home.

Leader When something wonderful has happened and I want to tell everyone…
All I turn home.

Leader When I'm confused and want to make the right choice.
All I turn home.

Leader When I've made a mess of things…
All I turn home.

Leader When I need to confess…
All I turn home.

Leader When I need to say sorry…
All I turn home.

Leader When I cannot fix the things that are broken…
All I turn home.

Leader When I am ready to give God my best…
All I turn home.

Leader When I am old and giving up more and more things…
All I turn home.

Leader When I am ready for my heavenly homeland…
All I turn home,
I turn home.

Amen

Healing the Land

Lord come and heal our land,
Let there be light in our darkened, soulless cities,
Let there be green in our wasted, industrial sites,
Let there be a letting go of our dirty, scarred, memories,
Let there be gardens in the ghettos of our church's story,
Let there be a loving for the soil from I which I came,
Let there be a neighbour in me for the nations of the world.
Lord come and heal our land.

Amen

The God Who Sees more

Lord God of signs and wonders,
When sin has silenced our song,
Sing about the good you still see
In us.

Great Son, friend of all who stray,
When shame has broken our best,
Create a new and living way
For us.

Wild Spirit winged with healing power,
When lies destroy our standing,
Remind us that you share this road
With us.

Therefore
We'll run,
Stagger,
And bow,
then kneel
In penitence
Because you care,
For us.

Amen

Resurrection Sunrise

When I cannot see the end of things,
When the darkness shines brighter than the sun,
When the wound will not be healed,
When I can see no answer to my questions;
Fill me with knowing you are there,
For me.
You are the first to weep over shattered lives,
The wounded healer who mends broken hearts,
The first to die and rise,
The holy victim who shouts through the silence,
"It is finished!"

When I am blinded by the power of present things,
Fix my eyes on you,
The battered God of the cross,
And break the power of my painful days
With reminders of new and better days
Still to come,
Your resurrection sunrise,
For me.
Amen

Remember Me

God of the dark and difficult places,
Remember me.
When forgotten,
When friends are strangely silent,
Remember me.
When foolishly I wallow
In broken dreams,
Remember me.
When I struggle
With the unfairness of things,
Remember me.
When I break and lose my way,
and rage and scream,
Remember me.
With my gifts unrecognised
And my life misunderstood,
Remember me.

Help me to see
The friends I do have,
Those who listen,
Those without answers
But who can hear
My questions.
Those who can touch
But not possess me,
Those not frightened
By the power
Of my doubting heart.

So weave the lightness of your love
Into the threads of my darkness
And do this in remembrance of me.

Amen

Healing Places

O God of all my healing times,
When I am rushed and racing through,
Find for me,
A place
where I can be still,
A time
To stay in touch with heaven's will,
A mountain
To climb above the things that bring confusion;
A garden
For dialogue and painful decisions;
A place
Where the hearing of your word brings visions;
A quiet place,
A screaming place,
A healing place
And a holy place.

Amen

God of the last chance

God of the last chance,
The next chance,
The only chance,
All — Don't let go of me;
Give me another chance

Son of the shepherd heart,
The broken heart,
The bursting heart,
All — Don't let go of me;
Give me new heart.

Spirit of the eagle-eyed vision,
The heavenly vision,
The nightmare vision,
All — Don't let go of me;
Give me renewed vision,
Through Jesus Christ my Lord.

All — Amen

Giftings for growth

O Lord God, Father in heaven,
Grant me those gifts which help me grow:
Your still small voice
Which brings me out of my frightened,
Closed down heart.
Fire of sacred love
Which heals what is mine so I hold
What is yours.
The Listening Christ
Who waits on my road of retreat
Turning me home.
Surprising grace
Helping me dig the precious pearl
From fields of dreams.

Amen

Christ before me

Lord Jesus Christ,
Holder of the heavens
Who spoke creation into life;
There was a time when you could not speak,
You have been down my road before me.

Lord Jesus Christ,
Walker among angels
Who rescued the bruised and the broken;
There was a time when you were carried,
You have been down my road before me.

Lord Jesus Christ,
Robed in glory, crowned,;
There was a time when you were hidden,
You have been down my road before me.

When I am speechless, be my living word,
When I cannot stand, be my strong support,
When I run and hide, be my one true friend.

Amen

Easter Risings

The Executioner's Art

Jesus waits
For the executioner's skill
To be delivered
In the silence of an
Effortless business drill.

The easy calm
of the craftsman as he carefully caresses the cross,
Checking where the victim's foot will rest.
His practised eye gauges the height
Of the man waiting for his finished work
And adjusts the stock to hold his body,
alive and dead weighted.

He tosses the nails over in his palm,
Measuring their length and picking
The best ones to pin his feet in place.
His patience is an art
And none of it is lost on
the battered carpenter
Who would be the first one
To taste his finished skill.

The killing calm
Of the soldiers, idling as they do,
Gazing at their prisoner
With a practiced dismissal;
Cracking jokes and lying as usual
About the women they've had.
It's their way of dealing with reminders
Of the disfiguring they're about to do.
After all,
They are only going to work.

The tortured calm
of the relatives
bunched together like stalks of corn,
Holding on to each other
out of nameless fears.
Feeling powerless,
dreaming impossible rescues.
And Jesus the victim,
is not silenced but still;
He is the only one
who has come to terms
With thc bloody mcss
On the side of the hill.

The Shapes of the Cross

Scream

What was that I heard you say
As you screamed at the God who
Had gone away?

Weren't you
Scarred long before the hill?
Deserted by your Peters
Supported by so few.

What were you thinking
As they bloodied you for more?
Was this worse
Than what you bargained for?

You dug deeper than most
When the beam slumped
Into the hollowed groove
Of the executioner's stump.

Nakedness

You hung naked
As the day you were born
But offered your Paradise home
To a thief bound and staked.

Like the emperor with no clothes
You were paraded with false praise
But I think you prayed for them,
Who gambled for your seamless cloke.

Powerlessness

Your enemies waited
Until it was hard to speak
When they poured out taunts
And dared you down from your peak.

Was it a moody silence
You were wearing
Or the steadied gaze
Of someone who knew more than he was saying?

Darkness

It was in the dark you did your best,
Instead of holding it all against us
You said forgive and
Your father did the rest.

How short sighted
The sight of you makes me,
Where I thought we had you caught
Was where you came to set me free.

When you pierced the air
With your finished shout
I thought it was all over,
But you had only just begun.

The View from Here

The view from here is terrific.
There are rank upon ranks of dazzling bright angels whose shimmering wings catch rainbows
as they glide before the ancient of days.
Mighty beasts bow to the punctured lamb
And heaven's holy warrior strokes the flanks of a purring lion.
Wise ones and golden unicorns hush heaven's wild party
When they fall before our shining Lord
And sing his praises and tell again the never ending story.
And I'm rubbing shoulders with Moses and Mother Teresa,
A Welsh bishop whose name I can't pronounce and a
School-teacher from Bognor I knew when I was eight.

You see further than your dreams have dared,
God is bigger than you have heard.
You can play leap-frog to your heart's content
And watch Jesus make straight everything that was bent.
The view from here is fantastic.
I've listened to hump-backed whales as they prayed,

Watched the lame as they walked around all day.
Laughed when the blind could believe their eyes
This is the place where all unfinished stories have better
endings:
The never born are named,
The unwanted are celebrated,
The forgotten are remembered
The aborted are baptised in crystal waves.
Together they sing songs that cheer the heart of the wise.
And guess what?
The other moment I bumped into that couple from
Our fish and chip shop,
And they're still smelling of crispy batter and hot, Pucka pies.

You can see further than your dreams have dared,
God is bigger than you have heard.
You can play leap-frog to your heart's content
And watch Jesus make straight everything that was bent.

The view from here is out of this world.
When you think of my final battles which left you low,
You should see what I can do now.
I'm not breathless anymore and I can scan a universe in
Technicolor,

I've got a radiant shimmer and a see-through glow that's to
die for.
I swim alongside star- fish
with names that you don't know
and I cuddle giant pandas
as we roll over in the snow.
I'm bursting with the pleasure of heaven's high lover
Whose hold on me has stayed my course
and called me so much higher.
I am seated in the heavens
and can see all the way home to you,
I'm kneeling with millions around a sapphired throne
And the sigh of our prayers is waking up worlds.
So be pleased for me and let me go
And when the angel trumpets your time to fly
Come and find me in the dance of darlings waiting in the sky.

You see further than your dreams have dared,
God is bigger than you have heard.
You can play leap-frog to your heart's content
And watch Jesus make straight everything that was bent.

Ending of days

Therefore, as the times of life go by you,
Deep peace of the ever present King be yours.

When you remember all those unfinished things,
Deep surrender to the Easter Christ be yours.

When good byes and endings are yours to say,
Deep words of the Holy Son be yours.

When the moment of letting go is yours to give,
Deep holding of heaven's shining Lord be yours.

When there is nothing else to say or to be done,
Deep speech of the one who says
"Come up here and see what must be."
Be yours.

Amen

Song of Saddleworth Moor

They tell me that your rage has kept you alive.
Are you sure that you are alive?
Your face is lined with aching loss
And each grieving cut weeps the question,
"It's not fair!
Where was God
when the children
were bundled into the soft peat
on the grimy rims
of Saddleworth Moor?"

Like a deranged animal,
Caught in a trap,
You lash and kick out at everything.
You cannot be comforted
Until you are done,
Until you have put it all down
And have told your darling child's story
And you finally know that you have been heard.

What compelling power and shocking beauty there is
As you bellow out in your pain and rage,
"Where was man, never mind God,
on Saddleworth Moor?"

Scored inside your heart
Is the unfinished song
of the never to be teenaged
Lesley Anne;
Whose dreams are long gone,
Stolen and broken and
Stuffed into the sloppy turf
Of Saddleworth Moor.

Someone's got to keep her story alive
But it has come at a high price.

Who will sing the songs of those who cannot?
Who will hold the remembrance of these things
When we have long gone?
Who will keep the wonders we hoped for
But did not get?
Who is there to stand upon the earth
And celebrate that we were here?

Who is there who knows where the hidden children sleep
In their unmarked beds
On Saddleworth Moor?

Only Jesus,
only the shattered son of the crucifix;
Bludgeoned out of shape,
Tortured and ritually disfigured,
Each segment of his abused cycle of dying.
watched over by unfriendly, distant eyes,
until he was silenced into the ground.
Who triumphed over the numbing anonymity of death
And delayed his resurrection destiny long enough
To terrorize and dethrone all the hopes of hell,
And emerge singing our silenced songs;
Picking us up where we had fallen
So we could join the chorus
And finish our songs around a throne of witnesses
On Saddleworth Moor.

This poem was inspired by watching a TV discussion on forgiveness between Gordon Wilson whose daughter Anne Marie was killed by an IRA bomb at Eniskillen, and the mother of Lesley Anne Downey, the daughter who was murdered by Myra Hindley and Ian Brady. Gordon Wilson had immediately offered forgiveness to his daughter's killers and it was this act of Christian grace which had triggered the rage in Lesley Anne Downey's mother.

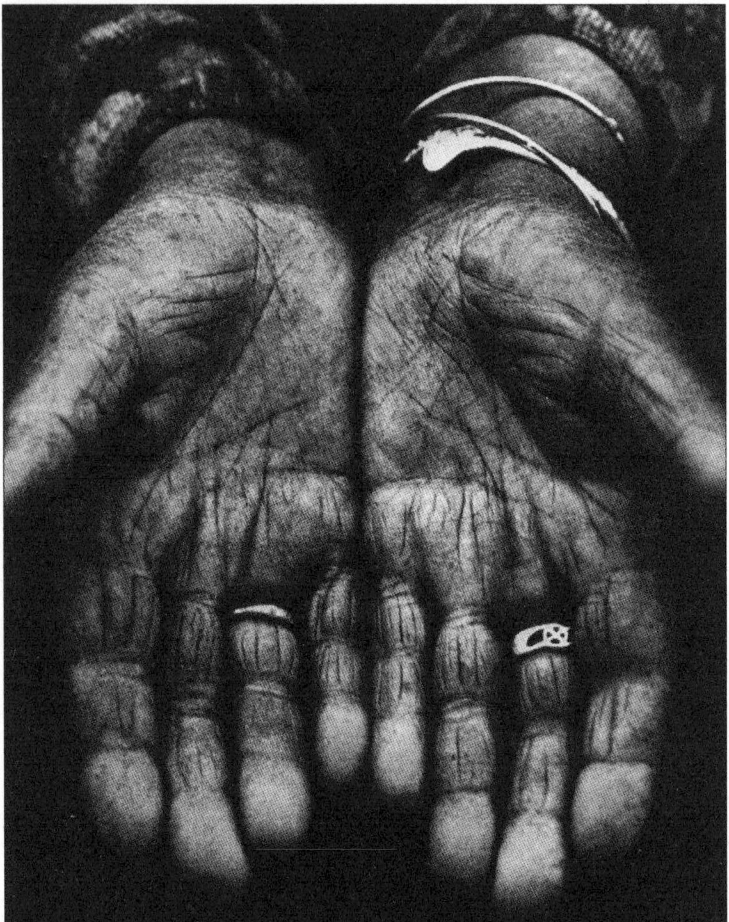

Hunger

Prayer for Holy Hunger

O God,
I have tasted your presence
And it has both satisfied me and made me thirsty for more.
I am conscious of my need for you,
But not conscious enough.
I am ashamed of my lack of desire.
I want to want you more.
I long to be filled with longing for you.
I thirst to be made even more thirsty.
Give me a glimpse of you
So that I will want to gaze for longer.
Show me your glory so that I may know you,
In your mercy begin a new work of love in me,
Get me out of my comfortable complacency
And be filled with desire for you,
In Jesus' name,
Amen

I Want!

God,
I don't want to play at being strong,
I want to go weak
I want to belong
I want to go low,
I want to be in the place where you speak.

I don't want deeply, meaningful absence
I want the irrepressible
I want disturbance
I want to go low,
I want the God of the impossible.

I don't want a tame holiness,
I want the wild Spirit
I want God's restlessness
I want to go low,
I want you to get closer than this.

I want
I want
I want you,
God

Give me Jesus

O God of everything that really counts,
I give to you my best;
The glossary of achievements which others sing out,
The shiniest miracle on which I dine out,
Possessions which I share out,
Blessings which your grace gives out,
My most important assets which I hold out,
Still give me the Spirit's power to want you more
So that I count all these as loss,
Only, give me Jesus.

O God of all life's challenges,
When I loose the thing I hoped for
Break the life I longed for
Squander the talent I was shaped for
Forget the dreams I was born for
Neglect the callings I was saved for
Drown in failures I didn't bargain for;
Still give me the Spirit's fire to trust you more

So that I press on,
Only, give me Jesus.

O God of all bright endings,
Whose stunning face we will all get to see,
And be dazzled by the daring of your eternity,
Where martyrs stripped of shape and substance
Are welcomed into their homeland haven.
Whose tiger-like, Calvary striped roar
Will deaden the assembled might of the hordes of Hell.
Whose return will clutter the sky
With air-born saints and congregations of angels
And blasting trumpets crescendoed
With some archangel's immaculate shout,
And even though I want it all now
Still give me the Spirit's passion to love you more
So that I eagerly await your appearing,
Only, give me Jesus.

Make it Loud

I cried aloud to God,
Not one of your controlled
and measured speeches;
But one of those loud enough
to make people think
you' re having a breakdown,
Or you're somebody
Who's a problem
and needs to be taken away,
quickly and quietly.

Don't give me this
"I am only a whisper away"
stuff,
I don't want to
gingerly spoon out
my heart to you
But scream up a tantrum
of needing you;

I have to get it out
and get it out still more.

Don't mistake this
for self-pity,,
Self-pity is a form of recreation
I am hopeless at.
I'm not feeling sorry for myself;
I'm giving myself a hard time
so I don't settle for less
Than knowing
the full blown version of you.

Amen

First Signs

When what I have will not do,
When invitations to pray
Feel about as appetizing as the shipping news.
When I'm tired with the God I think I know.

When I can't stand that latest
Everybody's singing it song,
When people go down in the Spirit
And I go out bored.

When testimonies sound
Like speeches at the Oscars;
When worship feels like I'm partnered
With a chorus of overweight dancers.

When I want to punch the next person
Who tries to fix me up and sort me out.
When I prefer sermons
To conversation,
When I smile too much.

When I prefer to be sceptical about miracles
And buy books written by mystics
But fall asleep reading the Forward.
When I can't be surprised any more.
When I scream, "God, there's got to be more than this!"

When there is no more fun in doing this;
Then it is time to get desperate for Jesus.

Amen

Just for once

Just for once,
Let's not have the type of revival
Which is more about being in charge again
Than about being broken open
And poured out in the care of worlds.
Rather, let it be the Spirit of healing saying,
"God is back
Giving the kiss of life
To a world turned pale and dull."

Just for once,
Let's not have that kind of worship
That's a search for indulging ourselves
Than about chasing after the illusive God
Who jumps on us from his hide and seek heart
And shows us little things to wonder our lives
And keep us chasing after him for years.

Just for once,
Let's not have that kind of report on the world's problems
Which robs me of my passion and reduces me to tears
Than the one that tells me how we are surrounded by
Lonely, angry, out of shape, hurting kids
Still waiting for the mending hands
Of a broken father's heart.

Just for once,
Let's not have that kind of healing prayer
Which makes promises of cure we cannot keep;
Or preaches illegitimate sermons
Detailing the shocking data of
Why healing has not come,
Than brokering a holy moment to listen
And invite a jungle of hurts
To untangle before the waiting God,
The embrace of the wounded healer Christ

Just for once,
Let's not have that kind of testimony
Which is more about revelling in colourful misdemeanours
With near-the-knuckle nuggets to excite us,
Than those stories of the Golgothared God
Who willingly traded our sordid and shattered stories,
On the butcher's hook of judgement,
So we could be reforged into his likeness
And carry the spark of God's renewing
Through the catalogue of the shifting years
To the endless pace of heaven's chorused dance.

Just for once.

Pathways

Waiting on God

In stillness,
Like the early morning air
Before the birds
Awake to dawning light;
In tempests,
Tossed about with angry moods
Teach me to listen
And discover your word to meet my need.

When I'm broken,
When I'm brittle,
When I'm confused,
When I'm cornered,
When I struggle
To find the right path;
Teach me to listen
And find the way forward from my need.
Through our Saviour Jesus Christ,
Amen.

Choose the road

Lord, bless to me the path I tread,
When I should stop,
Where I should go.
Help me to know
The time to be silent,
The place to scream.
Teach me to dream
So that I can sing,
As a child
Of the wounded king.

Amen

Invocation

Catch me God, in your generous grace,
Slow me down to your walking pace.
So that I might see you
Walking on my low roads,
Standing at my cross-roads.

Call me God, with your surprising hope,
Make my ordinary way a window for wonder.
So that I hear you say
"I'm here to restore you
I honour and esteem you."

Keep me God, despite my deep doubting,
Widen my horizon with new possibilities.
So that I know you
Shining through the everyday
Dazzling me with eternity.

Catch me, O God,
Call me, O God,
Keep me, O God
Through Jesus Christ my Lord,

Amen.

And God is greater than this...

I struggle with knowing that God loves me and it gets me down.
And God is greater than this

I have a huge temper and I wish I did not give in to it so much.
And God is greater than this

I battle with OCD and want to be a better mum.
And God is greater than this

I am a bad witness to the Jesus I long to serve well.
And God is greater than this

I am confused about what my role in the church is.
And God is greater than this

I am so easily put down and sink into my depression.
And God is greater than this

Invite more confessions...

Conclusion

O God, you are so immense and we so limited,
We can see only so far and you blink in visions;
Therefore we ask that when we stumble and fall
That you remind us that your love is so much greater
Than our capacity to fail,
And call us out of our dark shadowlands
Into the walk of your hoping light.

Amen

Prayer for honouring leaders

We lay hands on you today
Because we want to honour you
And say thank you for the gift
You are to us.
We recognise that it has not always
Been easy for you,
But we want to thank you for staying
With us and helping us to get closer to God.

We lay hands on you today
Because we want to say sorry
For not appreciating you enough
And failing to recognise your worth.
Please forgive us for not supporting you properly
Or recognising those times when you needed care;
For so easily listening to your critics
When we should have celebrated you more.

We lay hands on you today
Because we want to tell you that we are for you;
That we want to go forward beside you
And serve our great king together.
We realise that you too have your dreams of where
You want God to take us;
Some have been broken but some have stayed alive.
And so we lay hands on you now to say,
"let the dreams of God come true for all of us."

We lay hands on you today
Because we want your heart to be renewed
And your home to be refreshed by the presence
Of the high king whom you serve.
We honour you as the one whom God has definitely
Called to be our leader and cure of our souls,
We recognise that without you being here
We are not going to be truly whole.

So may the Lord of the church
strengthen our partnership
and take us all to the next level
of seeing his kingdom come through us,
his broken and blessed people.

Amen

Seldom do our church leaders have an opportunity to be prayed for meaningfully by their own congregations. This prayer is one in which our leaders, clerical and lay, along with their spouses, are invited to stand and come forward for prayer with the laying on of hands. Therefore the facilitator for this prayer would need to encourage as many of the congregation that wish to, to gather around and share in the laying on of hands.

Faithful One

You are the faithful one,
When we are faithless;

You are the glorious one
When we wallow in shame;

You are the forgiving one
When we have messed up;

You are the constant one
While we are so feeble;

You are the rock
While we drift around;

You are all in all to us,
You are our solid ground,
You are our heaven and earth,
The king of kings;

You are the reigning Christ,
The returning Lord,
You are the healing and delivering saviour
Who gathers all our confessions
and gives them a home.

You are the faithful one
Who turns our world around;
The Holy One
Who helps us dream again.

O most faithful God,
Thank you for believing in us
And for being there because
Without you we drift and fade
And loose the life for which we were made.

Amen

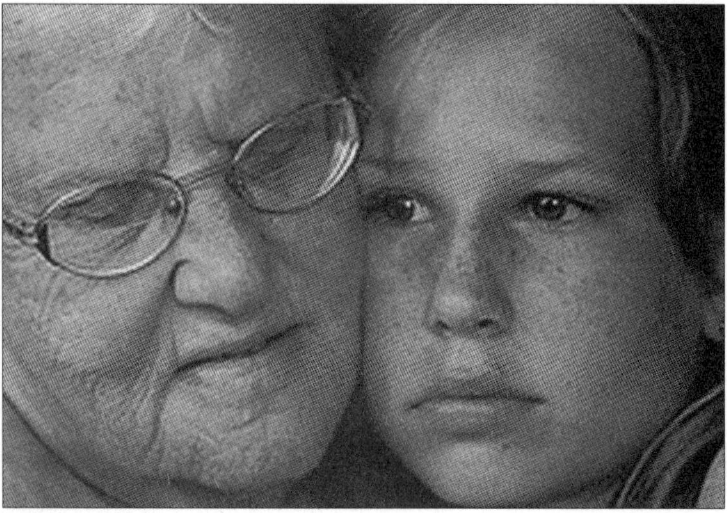

Rites of Passage

Litany of Invitation to Holy Communion

Leader Come to this place, not because you love God enough

All But because we want to love you more.

Leader Recognise that you are welcome,
Not because you have earned it

All But because our risen Lord wills it and wants it.

Leader Come lowly into His presence,
Not because God wants to put you down

All But because in due time Jesus will raise us up.

Leader Receive the healing touch of Jesus,
not because you are not well

All But because we want to live better lives than we do
And learn to give our gifts away
So that others may grow

All Amen

Prayer of Anointing

I anoint you in the name
Of the Father, the Son and
The Holy Spirit.
Send down your Holy Spirit on (name)
And renew his/her life in the service
Of Christ the healer.
Restore them in your love,
Encourage them with your power
And renew them in the father's image
Through Jesus Christ our Lord.

Amen

Confession for the Healing of Family Stories

Almighty and everlasting God,
Whose will it is to restore all things
In your well-beloved Son,
The king of kings and the Lord of Lords;
Mercifully grant that the family stories
We bring now before you
May receive freedom and healing
Through your most gracious rule.

Where there have been divisions,
Let there be restoration;
Where there are forgotten children,
Let them come home
And find more love in the
Father heart of God;
Where there has been evil,
Break the powers of darkness
And subject them to your righteous rule.

Let the power of your deliverance and forgiveness
Bring freedom to the guilty and
Renewal of life to us,

Through Jesus Christ, the first-born from the dead.
    Amen

Trinitarian Credal Prayer for Generational Healing

We believe in God above us,
Maker and sustainer of all life.

We believe in God beside us,
Jesus Christ, the Word made flesh.
Born of a woman, a servant of all
Who was nailed to the cross and died
For the forgiveness of everybody's sins,
Both the living and the departed,
Who ascended into heaven
And is alive for evermore.

We believe in God within us,
The holy Spirit of Pentecostal fire
Who is the life-giving breath
Of the church.

This one, triune God, brings healing
And forgiveness to all and His power
Is over the living and the dead.
He will come again in glory
And so we will all forever be together,
United with our triumphant Lord!

Amen

Creed for the One People

All We believe in one, holy, catholic and apostolic people.

Leader
We believe in making everyone safe and sound.
You love the differences in us,
You inhabit the edges of our ways and tears,
Our sharp and sensitive don't go there or I'll bust
Your face fears;
You tease out the surprise we can be,
You celebrate each human endeavour and act of kindness
Because that is when you see yourself in us.
You invoke all our diminished hopes
And bring them to full measure again.
You don't stop or give up on us until
We all come home together before the maker's throne,
To be cheered and welcomed as the returning children
Of the once lost family of each other.

We believe in making sure we stand on the same, solid
ground.

You swim in the uncharted waters of our hidden stories,
Live in our divided heartlands,
Heal the breakdowns in our border region lives.

We believe in not rocking the boat.

You're in the habit of shaking the foundations of the
world,
Turning over the tables of our well disordered priorities,
You say radical wonders that will be used against you,
You are often seen in questionable company
That puts you in the gossip columns of all our dirty
minds.

We believe in singing from the same hymn sheet, making
sure we are speaking from the same page.

You read books not yet on our shelves,
Sing songs that find their way into our dark and wounded
selves,
Woo us with holy whispers to dig us out of dug in hates,

Send text messages to guide us back to your homeland
heart.

When are we going to believe the same way as you?

When we breathe the breath of heaven's lion,
When we heal the wounded child in all of us o,
When we rediscover our capacity to be surprised o,
When we miss wonder and the ordinary,
When we stop playing safe,
When we are prepared to be broken open,
When we won't settle for less than the full blown version
Of you.

We believe…
We believe.

Creed for a Holy People

All
We believe in one, holy, catholic and apostolic people

Leader
We believe in being better than we are
And reaching out for the star
Of burning brightness
That leads us to the place of burning bushes.

We believe in being stopped in our tracks
And turned aside by God's sneaky distractions
Only to find ourselves on holy slip roads
Which bring us to our undoing by burning bushes.

We believe in taking off our shoes on holy ground
Providing that our feet do not smell;
We believe in fires that warm us well,
Providing they don't come with an archangel's
command.

We believe in mountain top transfiguring,
And ancient creed of surrounding heavenly hintings;
It's stretching it a bit though to confront us with the
    living dead,
And ask us to listen to what they have said.

We believe in Calvary mounts and hillside transformations,
And clues to the power of Christ's resurrection,
Providing we can stay awake long enough
And don't build our God-proof shelters too tough.

We believe that we cannot contain this too hot to handle
    God,
Who wakes us up to see that death has been robbed
And gives us glimpses of his glory
So we can make new the old, old story.

O most holy and overwhelming God,
Give us the desperate desire to be more like you.

You are the transfigured Lord.
Make us the transformed
Sons of Adam and daughters of Eve.

By visions of the tender, stroking lion
And the roaring, conquering lamb;
By watching the flight of burning ones
And kneeling at the sound of God weeping;
By knowing that when we are between
A rock and a hard place,
Or are in over our heads,
That you paid a huge price for us
That you would sell off the world to get us back
Every last one of us,
That you would trade your creation
To bring us all home to your heartland heaven.

We believe …
We believe.

Creed for a Catholic People

All
We believe in one, holy, catholic and apostolic people.

Leader
We believe in being the best dreamers in town,
We dream of a world where the broken
And the busted get to reign;
Where we listen to the sermons
Of the numb
And the altar calls of endangered species.

We believe in outrageous notions;
That all we do sings of God's breathing,
That God is so for the human race
That he puts up with our chosen,
Self-destructive sinning
In order to give us all the chances
We need to change direction
And find our way back to becoming truly human;
No wonder we need you Jesus.

We believe in a God who steps into our dreams
And calls us to strange meetings with other tribes,
Who troubles us enough with his love
That we take risks and live beyond our comfort zones,
Who calls the church to get off its assets
And find its true heart and then give it away
So others may grow.

We don't believe in God possessing us,
His father heart is big enough
To give us room to fight him off,
To tell him to stay out of our sleep
And say no to his mad grace;

We believe in the Great Son, Jesus,
The butchered blessed redeemer
Whose good news heart saves
All the desperate souls here;
The walking wounded,
The screaming and the silent,
The unwanted and unappreciated,
Victims and their perpetrators,
The wanderers and the waylaid,
The voyagers and the stay at home,
The dreamers and the damNed,

And those who feel they have left no mark
To say that they were here.

We believe in the wild, Spirit of God,
Who weaves the wind of God's new timings
Into the broken hopes of all our dreamings.

We believe in a God who patiently wrestles
With our temptations to settle for less;
Who won't let us wallow in self-pity
But tells us "You are worth much more than this!"
He only calls the broken to turn the world upside down
And insists that only fools need apply.

We believe …
We believe.

Creed for an Apostolic People

All
We believe in one, holy, catholic and apostolic people.

Leader
We believe in always being around as well as on the
move,
We believe in being absolutely still
And going for it when we can.

We believe in making our presence here as common as
dust,
As ever present as the air we breathe,
As committed as gravity,
As constant as News 24.

Then the world might know
We are here,
We're among them,
Mixed up with them,

Settled, camped and remaining here.
Unpacked and looking for room to live here;
Mulched in, dug over and manured in.

The sent out are we,
Wombling is our pedigree,
Underground, over ground,
wandering free.
We are the people of limited talent,
Broken, busted and bent;
Wondered by the king of dreamers
Emmanuel's peculiar race,
Ordinary people shocked with grace.

Not spiritual tourists on vacation caring
Visiting the reservations of lost souls
But pilgrims of the long haul God;
Not the passing through people
But the rooted and grounded in the soil tribe,
The ones who are here to stay.
This is our high calling
And if we live up to it at all
It is for the love of God,
For the honour of serving;
Because it must be this way,

For this way went our Lord
Of bloodied and bowed glory,
And because there is no other way on offer.
No new, big deal because it is the only deal.

We believe …
We believe.

Healing Death's Wounds

Rev Dr Russ Parker & Rev Michael Mitton

Since the tragic and dramatic impact of the destruction of the World Trade Centre on 11th September 2001, more people in the West are openly questioning issues of life and death. Before this, wholesale destruction of life was something that happened a long way from home. Now the wounds of grief are on our doorstep and they are felt keenly – both personally and corporately. Such enormous grief and trauma have led many to ask searching questions about the departed such as "where are they?" and "Will I see them again?" It is into these questions that our Christian hope can bring healing.

This book reveals what the Bible says about death and the departed. It teaches us how we can express our love for those who have died. It gives us an honest and fresh approach to the whole subject of what is the proper relationship between the living and the departed, and demonstrates how the love and power of Jesus brings healing to those who have been stung by death's wounds.

Healing Death's Wounds is a revised version of *Requiem Healing* and explores these deep questions of life and death. It offers insights into how to pastor the bereaved, foster hope in the faithful, commit the dead to God and deliver the oppressed.

'Michael Mitton and Russ Parker's conclusions, responsibly related to scriptural teaching, suggest that healing and wholeness for the living and the dead, requires a new understanding and awareness from people like myself, who peep fearfully out from behind the blinds of fear and prejudice. I know the writers of this book. Jesus is at the centre of their lives, and he is at the centre of this book too – opening doors, healing hurt and shining light into dark corners as he has always done.' – *Adrian Plass*

ISBN 978 0 86347 468 2

Free to Fail

Rev Dr Russ Parker

Since writing this book, I have been invited to speak on the subject around the world and yet I have not been able to reach the place where I have eradicated failure from my personal agenda. I still get ill – which is quite an embarrassment when you are the Director of a charity committed to resourcing the Christian healing ministry! I find it hard to pray regularly, I sometimes get irritated by the littlest of things, and I know what it is to mess up my life.

Yet through all of these blemishes on my heart, I am always confronted and made dizzy with wonder by the fact that God's love is never punctured or diminished by my failures. He goes on loving being there to love me, at all times and in all places. I do not wish to fail but am picked up always by the knowledge that my heavenly father cares and forgives and restores with a passion. So I am persuaded, still not to play it safe and be afraid of getting it wrong and failing, but to come out of such shadows and into the sunlight of his invitation to live.

Free to Fail extends this invitation of God to all.

ISBN 978 0 86347 636 5

Coming to God

James Borst

'No words can describe, no book explain, what it means to love Jesus' writes James Borst. 'We can only know from personal experience. When he visits our heart, it is bathed in the light of truth . . . Those who have tasted Jesus hunger for more. Those who have drunk of him are thirsty for more. But only those who love him are able to fulfil their desires – to know joy in his embrace now and glory later in his kingdom.

Coming to God, first published in booklet form under the title *A Method of Contemplative Prayer*, has already shown countless readers how to draw closer to God; how to drink in his love. They have discovered that it is a book to be pondered and savoured, practised and prayed.

This revised, illustrated edition provides a stage by stage introduction to a variety of ways of using times of stillness.

'I have read countless books on prayer but I come back time and again to Jim Borst's distilled wisdom. Coming to God is a book I would like to place into the hands of all who are serious about deepening their prayer life.' – Joyce Huggett

'My sisters and I want to thank you for giving us Jesus, the Bread of Life and his Good News through your words.' – Mother Teresa

ISBN 978 0 86347 635 8

Finding the Still Point

Gerald O'Mahony

Writing from his past experience of severe mood swings, the author provides a means to understand and govern the movements of moods and feelings so as to find the 'still' point – the place of perfect balance.

'Finding the Still Point' writes Gerald O'Mahony, 'aims to help the reader modify or alter behaviour patterns . . . It underpins common sense with the basic belief that we are God's children, and therefore not rubbish; we are God's children, and therefore not God.'

'Many of us have been taught to ignore our moods and to bash on regardless . . . this book clearly shows that to ignore our moods is to ignore the Holy Spirit at work within us and amongst us . . . Gerald O'Mahony . . . helps us to see that spirituality . . . is an activity in which we are all engaged, whether we like it or not, and which affects every aspect of our lives.' – *Gerald Hughes, SJ, from his foreword*

ISBN 978 0 86347 634 1